Images of Ilkley
in the 19th and 20th centuries

This booklet was inspired by Gilbert Lister,
the chairman of Ilkley Civic Society

City of Bradford Metropolitan Council
Libraries Division, Local Studies Department, 1982

ISBN 0 907734 04 9

INTRODUCTION

The earliest photographs in this booklet were taken in the 1850's when the population of Ilkley was only 811. (To-day the population of Ilkley and Ben Rhydding is about 13,000). The change from a small dales village to a prosperous community was accelerated by the popularity of Hydropathy, the coming of the railway, and the release of land to the south of the Grove by the Middleton family for building purposes — all occurring in the middle of the 19th century. Ilkley became a commuter area for businessmen working in Leeds or Bradford. These families increased the population to 2,511 by 1871, and it was they who were the foundation of a more outward looking community.

We have only been able to show some of the changes which have occurred during the last 130 years, but at the end of the book we show two fine examples of shop fronts which are to be found on the Grove to-day.

It proved difficult to draw a map (see back page) which would be a useful size, and still accommodate all the area. So the map shows the location of ⅔ of the photographs and for the rest we have used directional arrows. The numbers on the map refer to the pages in the book.

EDITOR'S NOTE

Thanks are due to Geoffrey Vere for all the modern photographs (with the exception of the two shop fronts taken by Mr. T. Haigh) and the overseeing of the old ones. In respect of the old ones we are most grateful to Mr. and Mrs. Burton, Mr. Harrison, Mr. Jackson, the Nudds Family and Ilkley Library (the Shuttleworth collection) for allowing us to use some of their photographs.

Thanks are also due to the committee chaired by Esme Greenwood who selected the photographs and read through the final draft, and to Mr. Townson for his assistance. Much of the textual information comes from the Ilkley Gazette. I wish to record my appreciation to the staff of the Ilkley office of the Gazette for their willingness to let me look through the original newspapers.

Finally we would like to express our gratitude to the Bradford Library staff, for their encouragement and support without which this booklet would not have been produced.

Eileen Mellor

Ben Rhydding Hydropathic Establishment was built in 1843 on the instructions of the Mayor of Leeds, Hamer Stansfield. It cost £30,000 and offered a wide variety of baths which were said to cure asthma, rheumatism, skin infections etc. Slightly further down the hill can be seen the farm cottages and stables belonging to the Hydro and further down still is the village of Wheatley.

BEN RHYDDING FROM THE "CALF" 1982
Ben Rhydding Hydro was demolished in 1954/55 to make way for a housing estate. Wheatley, now Ben Rhydding, has become a community in its own right, with its own shopping centre. The corner of the Golf course is visible and, just beyond its boundary wall can be seen one of the lodges belonging to the Hydro which was clearly visible on the earlier photograph.
The moor path has had to be surfaced, because of all the visitors who climb up to the Cow and Calf in the summer. The rock on the left is the Calf.

The road immediately at the bottom of the picture is the cart road used by the wagons to fetch stone from the quarry. Hangingstone Road was in a bad state of repair due to these wagons using it whilst laden with stone. Further down the road became known as Cowpasture because that is exactly what it was until it was opened up for building purposes in 1858. Cragg Dam, later to be enlarged and renamed the Tarn can be seen on the left.

ILKLEY FROM THE ROCKS, 1982
Stone is no longer quarried here. The quarry is used for rock climbing. One of the obvious differences between the two photographs is the wooded aspect of the area to-day. The roads are barely visible. The grammar school which was opened on this site in 1881 can be seen very clearly in the centre of the picture with its new buildings.
Middleton is now a developing area with the monastery still overlooking Ilkley.

This cottage was probably known as Todthorpe. It appears to have the living room and bedroom on the right and a barn on the left. Note the wood stacked at the left of the field. An interesting item of washing on the clothesline, is a pair of pantaloons. In the background are the Cow and Calf Rocks.

CONSTABLE RD. 1982
It is quite likely that the 3 trees in this photograph are the same ones that were in the previous photograph. There is no longer a farm here, although there is a barn (not visible) where the horse is stabled. The old roadway can still be seen (on the right) even though it is now inside the field.
There is the possibility of a house being built here again in the near future.

The Stoney Lea Hydropathic Establishment was built in 1883. It advertised a full range of baths, and had a recreation hall and a Winter garden. The proprietor was Mr. Emmott who had been a bathman at Ben Rhydding Hydro. As hydropathy became unfashionable the Stoney Lea became a hotel and catered for coach parties as well as private guests.
The roofs that can be seen over the trees are those of houses in Cowpasture Road.

TOP OF COWPASTURE RD. 1982
The hotel was demolished in 1981, planning permission for 23 flats having already been obtained. The houses on the opposite side of Cowpasture Road have changed very little over the past 80 years.

These buildings were part of Bolling Farm, later known as Sedbergh House. They were demolished in 1897 to make way for a library, but the land remained derelict until 1903. The spire in the centre of the picture belongs to the Methodist church, whilst the spire of the Congregational church can be seen on the right.

STATION RD. 1982

All this area was built on in the first decade of the 20th century — the land belonging to Sedbergh Trustees, who have a road named after them a little way up Cowpasture Road. In 1903 a library was envisaged, but then a town hall was deemed necessary, and then it was stated that no town the size of Ilkley was without an Assembly Room. On to that they then built an Annexe which became known as the Winter Gardens. They were opened officially in 1907 —- the Library being opened by Robert Collyer.

These cottages, at this time in a bad state of repair, were here at the beginning of the 19th century. They were used as shops as well as homes. Note the dog asleep on the stone front.

STATION RD. 1982
At first glance this view seems to have very little to do with the previous one. However the gates in the previous picture are thought to be the gates which led into the station goods yard in the 1860's.
The Midland Hotel was built in 1868, but the Station Hotel is older — its original name being appropriately 'The North View'. Shops have been here since the coming of the railway as this was thought to be a good situation for catching the day trippers as they left the station.

This view shows the original thatch cottages alongside the slate roofed houses. Lister's refreshment rooms were well known. The shop at the right hand side is thought to be a chemist's shop owned by Miss Batty. She moved to Wells Road in 1870 when this site was cleared in order to widen the road.

TOP OF BROOK ST. 1982

Dacre, Son and Hartley have their premises where Lister's Tea Rooms used to be, and Batty's chemist shop has made way for road widening and the fountain. On Wells Road can be seen one of the original buildings — now a shop, whereas on Wells Walk the houses appear very different. Some of the trees have been left to grow, so White Wells is no longer visible.

The millpond belonged to Thomas Lister whose house can be seen just below the pond. On the left of the photograph is one of two lodges of Wells House Hydropathic Establishment and some of the visitors can be seen horse riding. The ladies on foot are Mrs. T. Robinson, Miss Lancaster, Miss Ickringill and Mrs. Sunderland. The houses on the right — West View — would also have visitors who wished to benefit from the baths.

WELLS RD. 1982
The trees have now grown to their full height so that it is not possible to see the left hand side of the road. However the lodges are still standing and so is the flight of steps down to the pond. West View houses can still be seen through the trees on the right.

Trees have been planted on Wells Rd., and the Royal Hotel is very much in evidence with its three gables. On the moor opposite a few houses are visible through the trees. Mr. Middleton sold off this land in the 1880's and it became the responsibility of the Wharfedale Estate Company (formed from local business and professional men) to oversee the development of the area. It is now known as Middleton.

WELLS RD. 1982

All the trees survived and make for a very pleasant area. Now that there are so many sheep on the moor, a cattle grid has been placed across the road with a gate for pedestrians to use. It can be seen that the beck still follows its same course into Ilkley.

The Crescent House Hotel, or Rombalds Hotel as it will soon be called, now has its chimney pots.

This is the path from the mill into Ilkley. This mill was owned by Thomas Lister and when it ceased to function in 1868, he became the landlord of the newly built Midland Hotel. The mill buildings and house can be seen at the top end of the path. On the left is the new vicarage. The previous one was in Church Street.

MILL GHYLL 1982
The mill was uninhabited from 1868. In 1870 Mr. Middleton gave Mill Ghyll to Ilkley on condition that they preserve it as 'an arboretory with a clear and rippling stream'. So in 1874, "Fir, Laurel and Holly" were planted with a Hawthorne 'fence'; and so it has remained.

This is a Jubilee Celebration (1887) photograph taken from the top of Brook Street. The bridge is almost finished and is obviously safe enough for people to stand on. Umbrellas are being used as sunshades, although some parasols are visible. Everyone is wearing a hat. In the case of the men it seems to be a choice between bowler and straw. Ilkley's Town Band can be seen in the bottom right hand corner.

TOP OF BROOK ST. 1982

Scenes such as the Jubilee Celebration would be held, hatless, in East Holmes Field to-day. There is no longer an Ilkley Band, although there are various bands in Ilkley which could perform such a function. In 1966 it was decided that the railway should once more terminate at Ilkley and so the bridge was demolished. On the right shops have taken over from the railway houses.

The railway bridge had been in use for 40 years and was also useful as an advertising aid — Inghams having their office in a wooden hut conveniently near the bridge. The bus is travelling to Huddersfield via Shipley and Bradford. It was felt that double deckers looked unsafe. The car on the left is in a taxi rank. Hampshires had a fruit and vegetable shop below the bridge, but were not on this site in 1836.

BROOK ST. 1982

Inghams is no longer in business. Of the other shops in the photograph, Hampshires, whose sign is visible, is now owned by Almonds who still sell fruit and vegetables; Woolworths came in the 1930's and other shopping areas are signposted for the benefit of the many tourists who come to Ilkley.

The buses no longer run to Huddersfield direct — you have to change at either Shipley or Bradford. Taxis now wait on Railway Road, as, today, this part of Brook St. is a dual carriageway with so much traffic that a pedestrian crossing is necessary.

Brook Terrace, built in 1855, is on the right, with steps up into the shops. On the left there is only one shop, the rest are private houses and were shortly to have a small patch of ground in front of each house, fenced off with iron railings. Later the iron railings were removed and shop fronts took their place. Across the top of Brook St. the large shop sold fish, fruit and probably vegetables whilst next door was a shoe maker.

BROOK ST. 1982

120 years have made a great deal of difference to Brook St. No longer do you have to go up steps into the shops, and the balconies over Brook Terrace have gone. There are no private houses in Brook St. today, although many of the first floor windows are the same. Both footpaths have been paved and markings painted on the road for traffic. Trees have been planted, making the street look more attractive than in the 1860's.

Jesse Bontoft was a well known photographer. He took views of Ilkley as well as portraits. Behind his shop he had 'a pretty little greenhouse filled with specimens of palms and ferns'. These he used to give a suitable background to his portraits. Behind his shop can be seen a sign for G. C. Green. He was a whitesmith, which, today, we would call a tinsmith. He later opened an ironmongers shop on the Grove.

SHOPS ON BROOK ST. 1982

Silvio's stands where Bontoft had his gallery and the space used by the horse and cart is now a road. Mr. Green's workshop has been demolished to make more space in the car park. Shuttleworth's advertisement has been covered up by a block of shops, but the oddly shaped roof is still visible.

The farm, owned by Billy Hawksworth, was demolished in 1868 to make way for a street now known as Hawksworth Street. The actual farm house was bought by Shuttleworth, knocked down and Gothic House built in its place.

HAWKSWORTH ST. 1982

It is not possible to stand in the same spot to-day. Billy Hawksworth's farm would have stood where the out building belonging to the Fish Dish now stands. It would have adjoined the piggeries behind the Rose and Crown. To-day the parish church is visible between the Rose and Crown and its outbuildings.

Shuttleworth had a smaller shop four doors away, but then built Gothic House, 'the largest shop built or projected and (is) architecturally unique'. He was doing extremely well — not only had he a large fancy goods repository but he also had a station bookstall and printed the Ilkley Gazette and the Wharfedale Almanac. Apart from his stock of photographs he also ran a lending library – 10/6 a year or 2/– a month, for 1 complete book at a time.

GOTHIC HOUSE 1982
When Shuttleworth's moved from Gothic House in the 1920's, Mott's, which is remembered as a shop selling china, took it over. It then became the Thrift stores and now it is the Fish Dish with a completely new front at ground floor level. The upper rooms, however, are still recognisable as Gothic House. Supasnaps is also recognisable as Barnshaw's, although there are various window changes.

Both the Wharfedale Inn and the Star were supplied by Ilkley Brewery Company which had its premises on Railway Road. The Wheatsheaf Hotel on the left of the photograph was probably built in the 17th century as a private house. The Ilkley Gazette started life in the upper rooms of the Wharfedale Inn. The lamp post was one of the first in Ilkley and was lit in 1866. The post box was also a 'first' and erected in 1873.

BOTTOM OF BROOK ST. 1982

New Brook St. was in use in 1904. This meant that the Star and the Wharfedale Inn had to be demolished. It was decided to build a new public house to be called the Star-in-Wharfedale — thereby combining both names. It was opened in 1905. To-day it is simply known as the Star. The Wheatsheaf Hotel was seen by the authorities to be a traffic hazard in 1947, and so it was pulled down. The corner was later landscaped.

These cottages were up for demolition. Their place was to be taken by the continuation of Brook Terrace. The name over one doorway says Shoesmith and in fact he did repair and make shoes besides selling 'Mackintosh overcoats and leggings'. On the far side of his door the windows have been modernised — they no longer slide horizontally but are "modern" Victorian sash windows.

CHURCH ST. 1982

The row of cottages has given way to a row of shops which were built to match the ones in Brook Terrace, forming a continuing terrace. Only the difference in height (not visible here) shows that they were built at different times. This part of the terrace has, however, kept its balconies.

The traffic lights could never have been foreseen 100 years ago.

This field was used for Ilkley Feast in the middle of September. The Ilkley Gas Light Company had its original premises here, the chimney is on the left. Although there were several gas lamps in Ilkley in the 1870's they were always turned off for 4 nights before and 4 nights after a full moon and in any case from April to September. During the winter they were turned out at 11 p.m. On the right can be seen Ackroyd's tearooms and at the back is the curved roof of the Crescent Hotel.

OFF NEW BROOK ST. 1982
This area is very different to-day. Beyond the outbuildings there are more houses and fewer workshops and the old pathway is still visible. The gas chimney has been demolished, although the house chimneys are remarkably unchanged.

The Rose and Crown appears to have lined up its staff, clientele and one of its horses for the photographer. It was an old coaching inn, and coaches left Ilkley from here at 7 a.m. and returned at 4 p.m. They went to Leeds on Tuesdays and Saturdays and Bradford on Thursdays. Once the railway came, the coaches fell out of favour.

ROSE AND CROWN 1982
The Rose and Crown is still a lively public house. It no longer has stables and piggeries, but it prides itself on being the oldest public house in Ilkley. There appears to have been some reconstruction. The middle section has been built up to the same height as the left hand section, and the gas board building would seem to be a modern one. The chimneys, however, have remained the same.

On the left of Church St. can be seen a variety of shops, whilst on the right is the porch of the old vicarage known as the Charity Hole. This porch was used as a dispensary where Dr. Scott dispensed 'gratuitous advice to the poor' on Mondays, Wednesdays and Fridays 12 – 1. It was also used by those who went to the Bath Charity Hospital (now the convalescent home on the Grove). They were given 5/– a week from the dispensary to find themselves lodgings and food.

CHURCH ST. 1982

The left side of Church St. has altered surprisingly little. The tall building was erected in 1895. Although the corner shop is now a car show-room the window area is exactly as it was. The right hand side, however, is very different. The entrance to Hawksworth St. is visible on both photographs, which enables us to 'place' Beanlands Arcade (also erected in 1895) and see that it was built on the site of Lister's Tearooms. The overall architectural plan of the buildings making up the Arcade is very clear in the photograph.

Donkey Jackson lived in Bridge Lane and several of his donkeys can be seen in front of his house. He hired them out at 4d an hour or 'proportionally less if hired by the day'. They would be mainly used to take visitors up to White Wells to visit the baths and spring. The donkeys had a habit of straying and were threatened with being rounded up and put into the stone walled 'pound' if they were not kept under control.

BRIDGE LANE 1982
Donkey Jackson's cottage was eventually replaced by landscaping for houses which stand well back from the road. The houses on the right are still the ones built in the 18th and 19th centuries, although they have been modernised and give a brighter aspect to the road.
The trees which can be seen at the end of this road belong to Riverside gardens, which were laid out after the second world war to commemorate those who had died in that war.

Everyone has come out to have their photograph taken. The cottage on the right, at the bottom of the dip in the road belonged to Lister's who had refreshment rooms. Next to it is Box Tree Cottage and just off the photo on the right is the New Inn or Lister's Arms which was built in 1825. The road was the turnpike from Otley to Skipton and in 1874 a surveyor was paid £50 a year to see that it was kept in good repair.

SKIPTON RD. 1982

In spite of the transformation which has taken place, the church tower is still visible. The trees on the right hand side of Church St. have been cut back so that the Box Tree, which is now a restaurant, is clearly shown, as is the Lister's Arms.

The road is no longer a turnpike, although it is still a major road over the Pennines or into the Dales.

There were many complaints about manure heaps and their smells, although the very smart gentleman in the photograph does not look as if the heaps would be his responsibility. The turretted building on the left is the Grove Hydropathic Establishment. On the moor are some large villas. The air was considered to be drier up there than down in Ilkley as it was 'too high for the valley fogs that frequently settle over the village in the colder season' (Alderman Semon at the opening of the Semon Home in 1875).

CAR PARK 1982

The fields eventually gave way to a car park. This experiment was first tried in 1922. At that time white posts indicated a circular roadway for parking purposes. Private cars were 2/– a day (now it is 10p an hour) charabancs and heavy lorries 3/– a day or 2/– for 2 hours. It was fully supervised from 9 a.m. to 9 p.m. (the hours now are 8 a.m. to 8 p.m.).

Shops have been built along the Grove, backing onto the carpark so that the Spa Hydro building, earlier known as the Grove, is barely visible.

The Grove Ilkley.

The Canker Well was inside the public garden on the left. It was given to Ilkley by Mr. Middleton in the 1870's. In order to effect an improvement in health, it was recommended that the waters be drunk 3 times a day. The garden gates on the right belong to the Spa Hydropathic Establishment. The Grove was obviously a popular shopping centre with little traffic, which is presumably the reason for the car driving down the centre of the road.

50

THE GROVE 1982

The Canker Well remains although it has a more open aspect to-day. The creeper no longer covers the corner building, which is now an opticians, but the reception area still bears witness to the decorator's craft. The Spa Hydro has become flats and its front garden a private car park.

The area is just as popular for shopping, although there are far more cars.

The Congregational Church, unfortunately, is no longer able to be used because of deterioration of the fabric.

Chapel Lane was so called because the Methodist Chapel (built in 1834 and now Glovers Garage) was at the bottom of the lane. These houses were inhabited mainly by manual workers and the ones at the bottom of the lane were noted for having earth floors and being damp. Two of the houses further up the lane demonstrate the old economic method of adding a new house onto and above the gable end of the old. The posters show very clearly the rule that you could paper over another man's poster providing the paste had dried.

CHAPEL LANE 1982
The bottom of this lane has been demolished for the new flats and their landscaped grounds. The rest of the houses are still standing with the exception of the top cottage. This has been replaced by the buildings and grounds of the Baptist church whose gable end can be seen above the trees. Both sides of the lane now have a footpath, but the wall on the north side is much lower than it used to be.

This is one of several farms in the district of Ilkley known as Westwood. These farms varied in size from 45 acres to 245 acres (an amalgamation of 2 farms owned by the same family). This farm track was later named Parish Gill Drive, but it remained in this state for many years.

PARISH GHYLL DRIVE 1982

Parish Ghyll Drive has changed rapidly over the last 80 years. There are no farms now, but a number of Edwardian houses and a larger number of modern ones. White House Farm is the oldest house by about 50 years. The road keeps its rural appearance with its grass verges, its trees and the proximity of Panorama Woods which may be seen on the left, behind the houses.

These shops are situated at the beginning of The Grove. Note the canopy with the delicate iron filigree. Note also the interesting design of the bay windows and their roofs. They were built in 1899.

This shop, now a bookshop, was owned by Dinsdale & Co., wine merchants, as was the adjoining shop (not shown). Both entrances have mosaic floors incorporating the firm's initials, and each door has a carving executed by Mr. Eagle. The woodwork is mahogany which used to be stripped and polished by Coopers. The glass is the original glass.

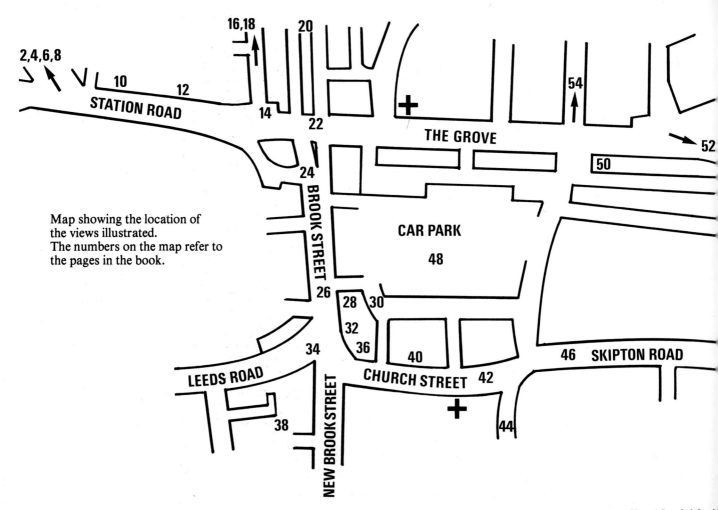

2,4,6,8

10   12

STATION ROAD

16,18   20

14   22

THE GROVE

54

52

50

24

BROOK STREET

Map showing the location of
the views illustrated.
The numbers on the map refer to
the pages in the book.

CAR PARK

48

26

28   30

32

36

40

46   SKIPTON ROAD

34

42

LEEDS ROAD

NEW BROOK STREET

CHURCH STREET

38

44

Printed in England by Elsworth Bros. Ltd.,Leeds